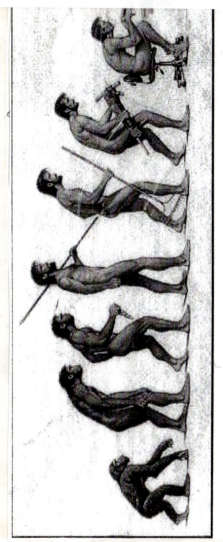

Pathway of Poems and Labyrinth of Lyrics

C.R. Paramesh, Ph.D.

Bloomington, IN Milton Keynes, UK
authorHOUSE®

AuthorHouse™
1663 Liberty Drive, Suite 200
Bloomington, IN 47403
www.authorhouse.com
Phone: 1-800-839-8640

© 2007 C.R. Paramesh, Ph.D.. All rights reserved.

No part of this book may be reproduced, stored in a retrieval system, or transmitted by any means without the written permission of the author.

First published by AuthorHouse 10/18/2007

ISBN: 978-1-4343-0400-1 (sc)

Cover photograph by Charles Kight

Printed in the United States of America
Bloomington, Indiana

This book is printed on acid-free paper.

Also by C.R. Paramesh

Fragrance of Life (poetic reflections) 1999
Leathers Publishing, Kansas-66211

About This Book

This book of Poems and Lyrics reflects original thought of an "atypical poet".

It is a conversation with inner self. Hopefully, the reader would get closer to the ones he loves and the ones loved and lost.

Some of these poems have appeared in Minotaur Volumes, in anthologies in US and on the Internet.

I express sincere gratitude to my friend and poet Jim Watson-Gove for his guidance and encouragement in my pursuit of writing. I am thankful to my friend Charles Kight for suggestions on the first draft of many of the poems. I sincerely thank my wife Dr. Jaya and son Hari for their support and computer assistance.

Contents

PATHWAY OF POEMS

AUTUMN LEAVES FLUTTERING   1
I COULD LAUGH AGAIN   2
COSMIC DANCER   3
FLY IN GRACE   4
SCARED ARE YOU   5
OH, BLESSED SOUL   6
CURTAIN DRAWN   7
PATH OF LIFE   8
GLAD TO BE SAD   9
AT SUN DOWN   10
MY GOD AND THY GOD   11
IF I WED THEE   12
IN DEAD GLOOM   13
MAKE OF ME A COMPLETE WOMAN   14
TERMINALLY ILL   15
GOD, I LOVE YOU   16
UPON THE DEATH OF MY SISTER 18
EULOGY FOR THE LIVING   19
DAMNABLE MOSQUITOES 20
OF GOD UNSEEN   21
A FLOWER IN BOUQUET   23
CANDLE LIGHT   24
WHEN LOVE IS NOT LOVE 25
LOVE IS WHAT I HAVE   26
HE FLED AWAY AS A LAD 27
RUN AWAY SOUL   28
WHO WAS WHO   29
SHE LOOKS AT HER FOLKS   30
A DEAL ALL TO MYSELF I MADE   31
MY MUSE   33
MY HOME PICTURED 34
TIME ALONE   35

UNTIL THE GANGES RUN DRY   36
LITTLE JOHNNY   38
FROM THE HOME OF THE BRAVE 40
POETRONICS 41
DO I KNOW YOU   42
I HAVE A BERTH   43
ONE TRUE LOVE   44
A ROCK NEVER ROCKS   45
I NEVER SAID I LOVE YOU 46
RITA'S RAGE 47
FIFTH QUARTER   48
ROSE IS A ROSE   49
SHE WAS DYING OF DYING   50
DEAD I FAKE   51
LUCKY TO BE WED 52
I LOVE NONE BUT YOU   53
SHE SAID IT WAS INTERESTING   54
AN AMERICAN ASIAN   56
ON THE DAY I AM GONE   58
IS IT A PHANTOM   60
THIS WORLD IS TOO MUCH   61
IF I COULD FALL IN LOVE   62
WHISPER, I AM SO RIGHT FOR YOU   63
LOVE ME OR NOT   64
SHE IS it, NOT IT   65
ODE TO MY WIFE   66
BIRTHDAY GREETINGS   68
WHEN IT IS NOT, IT IS   69
PSYCHIC AUTOPSY 70
I SPOKE TO GOD   71
DOORBELL COULD SPEAK   72
SOUND OF SILENCE   73
NEW YEAR JINGLES   74
BEAUTY THAT I AM   75
INTERNET WEDDING 76
WHISPERING TREE   77
I PRONOUNCE YOU   78
TIME SHALL FEIGN   79
ZEN TO FUN   80
DOORBELL IN DEAD DARK HOURS   82
UNTIL I MEET MYSELF   83

LABYRINTH OF LYRICS

DOORBELL COULD SPEAK 87
HAUNT LIKE A GHOST   88
YOU CROSSED A LIMIT   89
MY DAYS AS A LOVER   90
TASTE OF HEAVEN 91
ALL IN THE NAME OF LOVE   92
DIAL ME FOR LOVE 93
NEVER TOO LATE   94
WITHOUT YOU   95
LOVE IS SO BEAUTIFUL   96
GOOD MAN GONE WRONG   97
FELL IN LOVE INSTANTLY 98
MY HEART HAS SPOKEN   99
ONE SILLY MISTAKE I MADE   100
I'll BET YOU LOVE ME   101

PATHWAY OF POEMS

Pathway of Poems

AUTUMN LEAVES
FLUTTERING

Autumn leaves fluttering
Million dangling musical
Swept off their branches
By gusty southern wind

To the sound of dancing steps
My feet wade through
The leaf filled yard
Where a huge maple stands
A solitary leafless tree

The wind flies open
Window to my bedroom
Leaves tossed on bed
With many a silent hue
Weave a quilt of leaves

The glow of the dead
Every hue bare naked
A beauty for the eye
Gift of the dead leaf
A gift of life

Pathway of Poems

I COULD LAUGH AGAIN

I laugh with you
Each moment, lively or dull
Sit together and whisper
Eyes alone speak
Go merrily the distance
Far beyond the shore
Never tired or look back
Share all your dreams
Wild and dreary
With passion and love

My dream is small
But feels tall
You seem far away
Give me your hand
Lift me, take me slowly
Well into day of light

With you by me
My hope lights up
I could laugh again
You and I dancing
Lovers in love
On endless ride

Pathway of Poems

COSMIC DANCER

In the bustle of my birth
I forgot the joy
Of spreading my wings
Into mystery of this world

Destiny made it right
I was in hiding unborn
But I didn't drift in vain
From being to becoming

Dark clouds hovering
I could vividly recall
Viewing a sensuous sight
Of a sweet, young girl
Far on the pasture at play
Nestling down
In the bosom of a man
As if in lulled sleep

An espied magic moment
It was far too dear
To cast away in fear
Eyes turning inside me
Thought it insane
To smother their romance
Embedded in this was I
A cosmic dancer

Pathway of Poems

FLY IN GRACE

Destination
Miles and miles away
The royal road
Is but nature made
Unpaved, unmarked
Laid in no straight
Or curved lines
No hairpin bends
Or dead end

Flock of birds
Fly in grace unseen
The high ways in the sky
Over sea and the mountains
Gazing the stars in heaven
Daring the sun and wind
Never get lost

Days on end in flight
Never loosing sight
No door to knock open
Nor a crowd waits
With drum beats of wings
To greet tireless voyagers

Pathway of Poems

SCARED ARE YOU

Let me be the one
To say I love you fondly
You have been so good
To me for so long
Can't get enough of you
Could wait no longer

I am just being me
I feel my love, unquiet ever
Tough delight to unwind
Could you for a moment
Take my word for what I say
Let me in, not be a stranger

Loved you all my life
Journeyed together long
Where we end is yet another
Scared are you for naught

Let you be you, all unclad
Trust your inner voice
Thou shall not go wrong
Not loose sight of what we have

Pathway of Poems

OH, BLESSED SOUL

In romance are we
Slow to swell
Free to float
How be it
Any different
Seductive souls
Rising sun of sort
Soft and cool
Only to inflame
Our love to peak
Romance
Can strike again
Before night's end

You are in me
So am I in you
Two entwined
Aimless in space
My love is pure
Pristine and noble
Spontaneous
Come close
Fear not my passion
Lest yours quench it
That is not who we are
Our love is deep
Oh, blessed soul
You are
For ever, for ever
In my life

Pathway of Poems

CURTAIN DRAWN

A family man
Worked his way
Much wealth made
With kids shared

Love of his life
A genteel dame
Passed his path
For long years

Joy and grandeur
He knew be finite
Painfully bitten
By death of his wife
Lonely in a world
He unto himself
None to cuddle
None with to dine
No hand to kiss
Or hold in distress

A curtain drawn
Between
Body and body
Not mind to memory
Penetrable
Close for comfort
He wished though
Bygone blessed years
Of he and her were
A dream yet in progress

Pathway of Poems

PATH OF LIFE

Path of life
Begins with the end
End the unknowable
All but certain to end
While life pursues
The road to glory
With mystic elements
Of real and false
Faith and belief
Echoing behind life
That fades away

Pathway of Poems

GLAD TO BE SAD

Of death
What is it to me
I may go to hell
I am glad I won't know
I am glad I can't care

In life
One thing I know
I feel sad
When someone dies
I am sadder
I can't feel sad
When I am dead

Pathway of Poems

AT SUN DOWN

Up above the street
Over looking golf course
A concrete track meanders
Like a river measuring
One-half mile exact

At sun down
Young and old
Some with pets
A few elderly with
Cigarette in mouth
As if
To fuel their motion

A few walk clockwise
Others counter clockwise
A few jumped the cracks
On the track for good luck
Circling the path
Was not fun filled
But for the mind's mill
That spins and spins
The sins, ills and wills

Time after time
Count the cracks on tracks
To ease walk endless
As if seeking
The Light of Truth

Cycle of life is only
Half at best, the other
Is as yet unknown
Karma in creation

Pathway of Poems

MY GOD AND THY GOD

Thou shall not shame
What is in a name
Name is people's game
Game is to name names

Had it not been for name
Would I be
Who I am or became?
Would spring be fall
Fall be spring?
Friend and foe gone
Joy and sorrow one
All be one strong
Chant the same song

Had it not been for name
Or had I a different name
Would you have been my God
Who ever you are?
I called your name
No God arrived
Was it your real name
Or a pseudonym

God, if you needed a name
Why many a name
Causing chaos and confusion
Is it true, God
You have several names
Cause you had many rebirths
Centuries apart?
And gave new names
To your new squads

If you had one name at birth
Been the same for all
Won't my God and thy God
Be the same God with one name?

Pathway of Poems

IF I WED THEE

If I wed thee, sure
Two be one
For full love I give
I become one-half of one
Is this what you like
As lovers of a kind

I speak not for you
Nor can you for me
I could not feed
The kind of love
I know you need
To fill a void

If I wed thee
Do I fake a smile
Or bake a cake
I could not

I be in half split
Half, yours truly
For falling
Nay, failing in love
Half- broken heart
Half is half way to
Heaven or hell
I could not tell

Pathway of Poems

IN DEAD GLOOM

Traveled far and wide
Across the globe
In style and pomp
With resolute mind
Not in search of
Gold or silver
To fill a void
His love of nature

Heart loaded heavy
Of memories, images
Scenic drives
Autumn beauty
Music and wine
In mind frozen
Dreams dried up

A sad Sunday
He died a jaded man
Clenching a filled heart
With no word said
In dead gloom hour
Many a friend saw him
He could not tell
Tales of his travel

Many paid a visit
Not for tales untold
To bid last farewell
To a friend on journey yet
To another land

Pathway of Poems

MAKE OF ME A COMPLETE WOMAN

If you are a gentleman
Make of me a complete woman
Hold me close in your arms
Capture softly my lips warm
I want to dream every night
Feel your warmth alright
If by night, I lay shy
Kiss my lips tight and lie

If I would wake up from dream
"You never kissed me" I scream
Insist being a virgin unloved
Ask what it means to be loved
Was it a dream I never had
If it weren't, would I be sad?

Do I know how long
If you were mine
Be it too ever yours
Let not the dream of dream
Be just a dream
'Cause I love it, I love it
If from dream
Hundred years come I wake up
With my lips un-wet and numb
Let you and I
In divine grace, mingle
Forever to remain not single

Pathway of Poems

TERMINALLY ILL

Terminally ill
Sweet innocent child
Well enough to know
Not why or when
Far or near

Time not running out
I am
That is the way it is
Life I know little
Dead is life
Life is dead
No life to speak of

Prayers and miracles
Love and faith
Failed to intervene
Not this night anyway
Touched by death
In somber I fade

Tired of being tired
To wipe my tears
Stare at ceiling high
Heaven seems neigh
Life flees
Before I flower
Why me I do not ask
Is tomorrow here I raise

Pathway of Poems

GOD, I LOVE YOU

God, I love you
Millions world over
Wait for the sight of you
Talk of your omnipresence
You do not claim
Judge me not un-godly
For questions I ask of you

God, I love you dearly
Because I love myself
I believe in you
I have faith in me
Are you not a part of I
My extended self-state?
If you are not
I would invent one like you

You are forever present
In thought formless
You are my crutch
When in pain or despair
Could I not visit a temple
Hide from the vile world?

God, you are
As good as Godliness
As mystic as mystery can be
As omnipresent as seen
As omnipotent as imagined
As omniscience as surmised
As godly as conceived
As perfect as perceived
As great as treasured
As invisible as wind and air
As revered as worshiped

Pathway of Poems

All those said of you
If true
How do you cause misery
Unjust and sufferings
Or be indifferent

Lead me Right, Safe and Just
If you love me as you should
I still am young and open
For a better end with strife
That is the purpose of my life

Pathway of Poems

UPON THE DEATH OF MY SISTER
(Saraswathi Sachidanandam)

Upon the death of my sister
I did not give a part of me
Lost my nurtured soul
My heart was hers
Just for the asking
I grieved why she did not
A selfless idol
Kind and gracious
Her heart sincere
Her love abundant

Death came on a pounce
Her head slumped
She could hardly breathe
Her face was serene
She lay in new grace
For Him to embrace

How could I
Let her from us part?
Isn't her eternal sleep
An assault on us
Our dream and hope
Could I ever on earth
Be the same me
Call myself the brother
I thought I was
Designed by destiny

"O My God,
Wake her up" I screamed
Cried and cried in vain
My heart pounding
Until I felt her warmth
Of tranquil spirit
With weeping eyes
Sobbing, voice chocking
She is gone, forever gone

Pathway of Poems

EULOGY FOR THE LIVING

I chanced to read
Larry's eulogy
"I 'm glad you're in my dash"
Delivered at a friend's funeral

Birth– death is a dash
Pondered over the dates
On tombstone with a dash
Birth and death
Is but a dash
Dash------
Is but the life span
Beginning an end
In the beginning
Is not a single point
A continuum
Of life lived or fouled
Life missed, life desired

Dash------
Is but a series of
Molecular dots on dots
Of moving moments
Traveled to the present
With a finite end mystery
Where, When or how

Living a life of love
Good-bad, right-wrong
Here- there, then- now
Hope feeds on hope
A promise of future or not
Makes life on earth
An exciting experience

Pathway of Poems

DAMNABLE MOSQUITOES

Past midnight
As I start to doze
I rise to quell
Damnable mosquitoes
Sing cadence ceaseless
Unlike a lullaby

I veil my face
Not sound proof
They buzz around
Scan my body frame
For safe landing
Pick the best opening
Of my bald head or
Palatable part of me

I try to kill
They fly droning here
Fly droning there
Tease my tired body
Head turns to music
Hands clap loud
Up in the air
The more I miss
The more they kiss
Some are quick to fly
Some slow and die

Pathway of Poems

OF GOD UNSEEN

Of God unseen
Many of you "exist"
As guardians of religion
Tenants in Church, Temple
Mosque and Synagogue

I know you not
Yet I ascribe mysticism
Power, and define you
Limit your abode
More I do, more of you show up
Not more of the same unknown
More of the way I discern

Gods, do you vie with each
For power and territory
Do you greet each other
Is there a league of Gods
And a summit of Gods
To resolve seeming conflict?
Come out of your dwelling
Talk of kinship you all hold

You cause world's despair
Witness misery and disaster
Have mortals believe in you
Wherever, what ever
Name you take; Buddha, Jesus,
Shiva, Vishnu, Allah or Yahweh
Are you all siblings
Offspring of One Supreme God
You alone can answer
Of you I know less to say

Pathway of Poems

Of great warriors and lovers
Millions "live" in cemetery
Blissful of the turbulent world
Call it a quiet kingdom
Does joy visit their Holy Land?
Are they safer than yesterday?
Have their souls been restored
Unto what end?
Do you, Gods, vote for war too?
You take lives, young and old
Is it in wrath or cause of time?
Please say not "It was God's will"

Pathway of Poems

A FLOWER IN BOUQUET

Don't you know
What love is
Don't you know
I love you
Loved you the day I met
Love you to the day I go
You look nowhere
You seek no more
Open your eyes
Look at me
I am the one
I am the one hunted
Until love meets love
You are a loner
I am alone
A flower in bouquet
Of your lonely heart

Pathway of Poems

CANDLE LIGHT

So beautiful
A bolt of glow
Lights up the world
Inside and out

Graceful witness
In joyous wedding
Add fragrance
And ambiance
To wine and dine
Spark lover's flame
To go it all day long

Turn night into day
Reach the hearts
You lit the place
Kindle the sprit
Of vigil on land
For souls missing

In final good-byes
Bowing of heads
You weep and mourn
Burn bright light
Stand a fraternal guard
Until farewell song

Kind-hearted
You heal all wounds
Bond broken hearts
You bleed in wick
Unspoken in praise
Turn off in grace
Under fire
Die yourself
For love and peace

Pathway of Poems

WHEN LOVE IS NOT LOVE

Ask me no more
What love is
Or how love means
Is love not love
If not given
Shown or known?
Given hug or kiss
Gift of a diamond
Or a red rose

Is love not love
When not shown
Vivacious interest
Spoken or unspoken
"I love you"
In words or verse

Is love not love
When not known
Deeply or subtly
As a mystic moment

When given it is done
When shown it is gone
When known it is old
It goes untold

Love if reciprocal
Comes of thought
Love reciprocated
Is but solicited

With body dead
Mind and soul wed
Love I must
As thou did just

Pathway of Poems

LOVE IS WHAT I HAVE

Love is what I have
True love it is
My love is deep
My heart does weep
Have I a place in you
Speak not in haste
Look at it unfold

Love is what I have
Abundantly I gave
You know all
I did or meant
That wasn't said
Or said wrongly

Hide not the depth
Of your love for me
Did you forget
What it is to be you
What you were to me
Time would light up love
That wouldn't be dead
In my body laid to rest

Pathway of Poems

HE FLED AWAY AS A LAD
(Raghu)

On a fair sunny day
He came our way
Joy and delight
Fun and laughter
Had not us known until
"Thank God", we said
If He had listened

He turned sixteen
Life was blossoming
Guitar was his passion
Led peers with a vision
He couldn't rest
Until being the best
Met many a hope
Desire and dream
Yet any unmet
He could not take
In a few brief years
He fled away as a lad

God gave him to us
Yet gave him not
Why in the name of God
Asthma took him away
Day after day, we mourn
In chorus of his music
He remains sixteen
For ever in our hearts

Pathway of Poems

RUN AWAY SOUL

I will call myself dead
If it weren't for you
Strangely though
You are neither alive
Nor are you dead
Poets long for you
To breathe their song
You appear, reappear
Migrate or transmigrate
Soul to soul, poet to poet
Who ride on you quiet

You live the longest
In brevity albeit
As shadow that I know
Substance I not see
Transcending
Time and space
A run away Soul

Ever in sound slumber
Never do you betray
Poets who love thee

Unborn yet eternal
You never die it seems
In poets' verses
Long after poets are dead

28

Pathway of Poems

WHO WAS WHO

I slumbered deep
Lie in wait
Holding my eulogy
I presume
I was dead
I could not tell
Day or hours
Where I was
When I was
Or who I was
Somebody
That I knew
Who
I was

I guess
I was alive
Words unspoken
Between Me Dead
And Me Alive
Blissfully nonetheless
Never knew
Who was who

Pathway of Poems

SHE LOOKS AT HER FOLKS

Just a year old
A delicate daisy
From a foreign land
She did the flying
Over the Atlantic
Until a New World
Sprung upon her life

Had not seen much
Of light or life
All a blank mind
To grow and rise
As the days go by

Day was still awake
Night had not gone asleep
Three in the morning
Of Christmas Eve, 1993
Our eyes wide open
Await the infant

Balloons of welcome
Dazed her eyes
Smile infectious
At midnight hours
She was ready to roll
Climbed the long stairs
Looked back for a nod
Up a few more steps
Sought another nod
A few more to the top
She looked at her folks
Down on the lobby
As if to say, "I am one up"
In the home she touched

Pathway of Poems

A DEAL ALL TO MYSELF I MADE

A deal all to myself I made
Standing mystic and puzzled
If I love myself for who I am
Or scared to ask if I am, am

Laden with all that I am not
Lost and lonely in an alien world
If I wake up to face my failings
And the weight of worthlessness
Would knowing these sadden me
I am all that I am not?

Who then am I?
Withering flower in wilderness?
Body and soul in darkness
Groping in search of *Nirvana*
Is my soul hiding in shame
Or am I hiding from myself?
An invincible twin
Struggling within and without
To touch, feel and cry out

Do I dare to leave my body
And look at myself as *maya*?
Could I secretly speak to myself
Still hold me at sanity's brim?
Open the doors for me please
I may sense the kind I am

Pathway of Poems

Do I know how to be who I am not?
Unleash my feelings of pride
Shame, hatred, and fear
And bring in me compassion
My heart filled with sublime love
To see yonder ere my soul withers

The best of me is yet unborn
A little pause is all I seek
Would I not in the end be
Who I really am
A mortal body bearing the burden
Of a stoic mind with conscience

I thought I could not be
Myself and I
I think I am
My journey is ending
With a pause for a beginning

Pathway of Poems

MY MUSE

My muse is to amuse
Not to confuse or infuse
Not impose just suppose
Ungraspable but gulp able
Not drain the brain

Why say no, let mind go
Where it does
More or less free of mess

Prose or poem
I have no qualm
To rhyme is prime
Not to rhyme is no crime
Is short less of an art?
You sort I part

Pathway of Poems

MY HOME PICTURED

Not far from the city
Across the sea
Far into horizon
My home pictured
Off the shore

Waves of water
Never ceasing to break
Rise as palpable tide
As my eyes take a ride
Lone man in space
See a blue curtain afar
Where I meet the stars
Collide in the sky
As I with memory

Consumed in rapture
Beyond the waters way
My home
A little run down
Walls filled with pictures
Stare at stillness
Of waters edge
To Gateway of India

Pathway of Poems

TIME ALONE

Mid-summer vacation
Another Sunday morning
She asked for
Time alone
To be with herself
For no known cause
To kids and family
Sad it would be she knew
It was no less easy
As the night was folding

Visions of little kids
Their love and memory
Filled her aching heart
As death was creeping
In slow, unkind pace
She hardly could sense
Or it was too late to mend

Cloud-like smoke
Hovered her numb body
She could shed no tears
Over come by near end
As sorrow befalls
Breathing feeble
Time was her enemy
Time alone stays, ticks
She lay motionless
Arms stretched
As in silent prayer

Pathway of Poems

UNTIL THE GANGES RUN DRY

Speak no more of her sweet voice
Radiant smile and sparkling eyes
Beneath hides a shining splendor
Of inner beauty that lit my heart
It did not happen at home or on a sojourn
I am glad no wise man can discern

I adore dearly her silken face
As I did at sweet sixteen
O! Happily, praised her by a verse
Raised even a garden of roses
Dared to wait for a precious kiss
She never stopped by to say, "I love you"

Haven't I been a stricken star?
In wait for her to heal my scar
She sure would come by moonlight
Hold my heart throbbing for her sight
If she would kiss me million a minute
Fate shall mandate dance in delight

Youth and romance slipping away fast
Do I tell her "goodbye" at last?
I wake up from blissful dream
In ecstasy to the perfume
Of bed strewn of jasmine
Be lonesome, senses part fading
Still look tired of tears I yelled,
"You, damsel, where the hell are you"?

36

Pathway of Poems

She gazed; the roses on her cheek
Were blushing, fresh and unique
Am I to feel loneness of farewell?
Is there any one around
Oh, no, I would see her
Feel oneness, soul on soul
Give her pearls a wash of purple
So wrapped was I, little did I know
Where I captured her grace
Ever to shine
Until the Ganges run dry

Pathway of Poems

LITTLE JOHNNY

Little Johnny
Is no phony
He is too much
Mommy is no match

Big Johnny is out.
Little Johnny shouts
Yells and pouts
Stings like a bee
Cries like a baby
Feels he is the victim
Too much for mommy
Pain and a pleasure
Beyond any measure
To the end of tears

I wonder if
He is a little boy
Teen or man
He is rude, silly and
Bully at the same time
He seems to like it

I can't speak to him
I have exhausted
All my incentives
He needs to shape up
On his own will
Or else others will

Pathway of Poems

How do I love him
Love I must, I will
So he must
So will others
Why do I love
Because he is
My Son Shine

Pathway of Poems

FROM THE HOME OF THE BRAVE

Touched by
Patriotic passion
It was a calling
To defend my country
Neither you mom, pardon me
Nor even God would
Hold me from
What I believe in

What today brings is
Tomorrow is unknown
No danger or doubt
Dared to haunt me ever
Should I in battle die
You will, mom, hear
My voice from grave
To wipe your tears
Of joy, not sorrow
From the home of the brave

Exultant be in pride
I was your son so long
Is there a greater honor
I could seek
I shall never have fallen
Died in vain pursuit
I bled for
My country I loved
More than my life

Pathway of Poems

POETRONICS

It just happens
Known in the heart
An impulse of delight
Gushes in mind
Restless and struggling
In disquiet harmony

Mid-day or mid-night
Awake or in sleep
Perhaps on a highway
Tune to the call
Of a chorus of words
Waves of thought

Not sure of what you do
Not pause for diction
Meter, rhyme or reason
Feel not the urge
To state a great idea
Or something lofty
To embrace
Stirred up feelings

Now you see, now you do not
You let it flow unfettered
Weave and spin
In the depths of your mind
Feel joy
In the stillness of your find

Pathway of Poems

DO I KNOW YOU

Oh, dear, I admit
I was upset
I never thought
You would doubt
My love ever
Why probe my dreams
I hoped I knew you
Enough to dream

I have all I want
When you with me
Do I mean the same
Does my love miss
Something you care
Beyond my telling
Tell me before
My living is done

How sad it is
Being lonely in death
I love you dearly
To want you by me
This one time I ask
Do I know you?
Thou shall get away now
You have unfinished work

Pathway of Poems

I HAVE A BERTH

Below the earth
I have a berth
I was dead
Descended gently
In custom made
Mahogany bed
Excellent body
With pink velvet
Star studded walls
Too bright for eyes
Water proof
Air tight
Can't breathe
Whisper proof
No voice heard
Sweet solitude

Cul-de-sac like
Dead end of sort
No traffic sound
Dead silent zone
Dwell safe alone

Full moon day
Or New moon
Sun rise or sun set
I can't figure out
My senses are sealed

Albeit my delight
It seems not right
For one done well
A full life cycle
To take a piece
Of earth of the living
It is time to move on back
To blend with nature
Wind, water and fire

Pathway of Poems

ONE TRUE LOVE

I had a crush on you
Your charming smiles
Calming moods
Held me long while
I traded the dawn
For your beauty
Nights as parlor
For day-dream
Days for night-dream
Rendezvous

Your heart and mine
Two sides of a coin
Neither knew
Other's pain
I quipped
Show me a man
Who wouldn't fall
For a dame like you
Show me a man
Who wouldn't care
For a dame like you

Your feelings swell
You know what they tell
You held my hand
I felt grand
Could kiss you fondly
But you beat me soundly
Now two hearts beat
As one true love

Pathway of Poems

A ROCK NEVER ROCKS

Rocks piled up tall
One upon the other
Big on small
Small on big
Dependently independent
Barely cling neat
Fashioned gigantic
A rock that never rocks

A perfect peak
Nature shaped
Buckled together right
Far off railway track
Standing alone still
Bounce blazing light
It seems to chase me
I can't believe it

A forsaken rock
Honeydew-drop like
Whence it fell
None could tell
I could, as I ask
Why did it speak
To me its make up

Pathway of Poems

I NEVER SAID I LOVE YOU

I never said, "I love you"
If I could, I would have
I did not tell you how dearly I love you
One of a million, I love none but you
How the heck it slipped my mind
I never said, "I love you"

I would not have said it right
If I could, I would have
Did not know how to unlock
Without a key my hidden feelings
What on earth had I been thinking
Building biceps, crunching belly at the gym

Every time I tried, I seemed to choke
Standing like a zombie, mesmerized
By your voice and sparkling eyes
Perhaps scared fearing the worst
So wrapped up, lost in romantic fantasy
I never said, "I love you"

Don't you recall
How often in pain and pleasure
When I was young and miserable
I leaned on you with tears for comfort
You made me laugh, forget my sorrow
You let go of any bickering or argument
You were there for me if only I asked
Yet I never said, "I love you"

If you could look into my eyes
You would know the real man I am
Man you would love to be with
I believe the by gone years
Were dreams in progress
Seeking a fine dame like you.

46

Pathway of Poems

RITA'S RAGE

It was
A bewitching beauty
Of penetrating eye ball
Closed with brilliance
And rainbow colors
Of Nature's choice
Peering at the land

But her fury and
Howling surface winds
Travel fast with
Sad, mean currents

It is a deceptive delight
In destructive force
Unlimited on the
Brink of explosion

With roaring sound
Strength unabated
It dashes to shore
Makes a landfall
Rests on earth's lap
Unwinds a little
With torrential flood
Before she fled

Pathway of Poems

FIFTH QUARTER

If you could
Stand apart from you
Place time in limbo
Be a spectator
Not of life after or
The one gone before
But behind the four
The fifth quarter
An enigma of life

Make sense soon
As darkness befalls
With or without your call
Look at events of life
Absurd and trivial
Faith, vagaries within
Memory dormant
Perish all, body as well
To pursue Truth
Count the pulse
For what it tells

Pathway of Poems

ROSE IS A ROSE

Rose is a rose
By any name
Rose dies today
Yesterday's bud
Blooms today
Rose it is
Rose is a rose

God made rose
Rose it is by any name
Is God a god
By any name
Could He still be
God by many names

Take Him at his word
Or should I be
Scared to disbelieve
Is my God a valid God
Is it
A mischief of mind

Is God
The best invention
Man ever made
As claimed by some

Why, I could not tell
How, you cannot spell

Pathway of Poems

SHE WAS DYING OF DYING

World stumbled
Spun into waters
Of the ocean's fury
The Tsunami swayed
She met her near death
Hanging on to a tree
Hours and hours on end
Watching wicked waves

Washed ashore herself
On ocean's edge
A solitary tree
She hugged tight
Was her only crutch
Bed and anchor
All drowned but she
The tree and ocean

Hanging alone tough
Terrified and dreadful
Fate turned cruel
Swept her lover away
Deep into another end
Her heart locked in him

Death was her only mate
She was dying of dying

Sanity departed
Stuttering to herself
Listened if she breathed
Standing atop the tree
Her soul rolled safe
By and by into body

This moment she knew
It was her time to live

Pathway of Poems

DEAD I FAKE

Devil chasing me
Down the dark alley
All the way
I run and run in fear
Not a second slow
Or a yard less

Where the devil is devil
I can't see a thing
I fear the thought
As real as real could be

I hasten to the end
Only to hit a hole
Do not know if
It is in or out
I fear the worst
Shiver and tremble
Dead I fake
Live, I would not make

Devil tramples past
I dread to wake
I dead sacred
Wake me if you would
I had no fear when born
Why fear now if dead
Do not know what
Goes on the other side

Pathway of Poems

LUCKY TO BE WED

Lucky to be wed
I would be fed
I have no debt
Until this I said

Being alive
Is a gift of life
Not to speak of wife
Lucky to be wed
Keep alive a smile
To go many a mile

Just for today
Love me, hold me
Tomorrow is a promise
Yet to be met
Blessed am I not
Flower in your heart
So full of you
I listen to my heart
Just to be by you

Pathway of Poems

I LOVE NONE BUT YOU

I fell in love with you
Yet, I have been alone
Why are you so distant
Any thing going wrong
That I don't know about
I wait for an answer
I won't say I will die for you
I live for you

I am not sure
What happened
You and I seem to be
Moving away from each
Have you someone else
If you are tired of me
I will back off for a day
I love none but you

I am a good sport
No hard feelings to sort
Unless you have some
I love to live for you
I want a fresh start
Following my big heart

You are more beautiful
Than ever; I can't say
The same about me
Shove me somewhere
Anywhere in your heart
I will gladly
Take it to my heart

53

Pathway of Poems

SHE SAID IT WAS INTERESTING

A dear friend of mine
Read my poem and
She said it was...*"INTERESTING"*

You are the word!
I look forward
You come in handy
Without being dandy
Opined not hastily
Nor thoughtfully
Neither sell nor buy
Just fill a void sly
It is by *Interesting*
You make truce
Between Thou and I

Friendly to foe
Mindful of woes
Say the least
Pay the most
A Convenient concord
Not jump out nor mute
Cause no pain, solace
Subtle, silky and artful

I can not smell
Feel full yet dull
Voice never wrong
Fresh as truth strong
Never alone
Any would own

Pathway of Poems

Elusive as beauty
Not a peach
May be an onion!
Round and round
Feel it, peel it
See many colors
Of autumn leaves
You said it all
With nothing said
That is thou
So is INTER e-STING

Pathway of Poems

AN AMERICAN ASIAN

America, a dreamland
I came to blend, not mend
Manipulate or exploit
Greatest nation on earth
Fearless and flawless
Undismayed, indomitable
A mosaic of many
Culture and climate
Religion and race
Language and peoples
Beneath all only one
Defined character
An American Asian
Not a hyphenated
Asian- American
Shouldn't the rest as well
Be called as such

Imperfect?
Where is the nation
I visualized?

Now a little saddened
Speechless and somber
Bring back your glory
Of English language
Character and guts
All seem anemic
I look to my country
The America I knew
I came to adopt

Pathway of Poems

You still are the best
One nation under
One Supreme God
One people of peoples
One language of languages
One culture acculturated
One character blended
Indivisible, free and fair
With liberty and justice for all

Pathway of Poems

ON THE DAY I AM GONE

On the day I am gone
I would not be sad
I would go in style
Not lay naked
But in cascade dressed
Layers of love upon love
A full life
I carry to my grave

On the day I am gone
The clock would strike
The ice would melt.
Sun sets, moon shows
Day dawns, night folds
They stay for you dear
I go

On the day I am gone
I can't comfort you
Dear children in sorrow
Sorrow for
What you miss
Sorrow for what I miss

On the day I am gone
I have no grief or rage
Rage at being gone
Grief at being born
Long after I am gone
You will see me
Love all you
Hear me yell
Same temper, unmasked

Pathway of Poems

On the day I am gone
I have a lot to carry
Would there be room for all
What of my name and fame
Degrees and diplomas
Books and bouquet
That comforted my living
Does it in Death

On the day I am gone
I shall flood my soul
With verses of thought
Memories of you
As in wake and dream life
You be all happy
With memories of me
Good to each, love bonding

Sorry I could not tell
Death was punctual
You know nothing good can stay
So I go

Pathway of Poems

IS IT A PHANTOM

Life began alone
Not really lonesome
Seemed painless
Warm and quiet
In mother's dwelling
A life of my own
Sensual and sensuous
Subliminal rendezvous
Never knew my name
Or my play beyond
Upon birth

Strange it is
Lonely in crowd
On this vast land
Free, full of men
And material life
They now seem nothing
Unless something of sort
In nothingness I see

Is it a phantom
Of bliss in pursuit

Pathway of Poems

THIS WORLD IS TOO MUCH

This world is beyond me
I don't belong here
Not the world I knew
But one I love to hate

The world I knew
Was gentle and reverent
Never made me feel old
A world it was full of spunk
None left behind to flunk
I was a happy camper

It has gone far ahead of me
I struggle to endure
But I want to know how
To feel I belong here
This world is too much

Ironically it is an exciting place
Where life is an exotic race
I wonder what purpose
Still remains in my defense
To revel from present pain

Do I take a step backwards
And get a new life, reincarnate?

Pathway of Poems

IF I COULD FALL IN LOVE

If I could fall in love
If I should
Who could it be
Who should it be but you

How could two of us
Be close yet so apart
So lonely, I know not
Loved you for eternity
You grew up with me
As did my love for you

You came into my life
Praises I showered
I could, I would die
Just to be with you

I do not take
Loving lightly
Gave all but one
Lovelier than ever
You may treasure
I did not labor long
Not a small heirloom
Better yet my aching heart
That holds you within

If I could fall in love
If I should fall in love
Who should it be but you

Pathway of Poems

WHISPER, I AM SO RIGHT FOR YOU

Whisper softly to me
Lest our pillows hear
Our dream's ambition
Not known to any

Is it love
At first sight
Or on first night
Say if you must
Whisper your dream
How in secret we met
In quest of first kiss
Our hearts never missed

Haven't our souls met
In pain and pleasure
If love is elusive
Fancy fleeting
Capture my smile
Before it smothers you
Let us live today
Tomorrow is too distant
I am so right for you
Are you not for me
Speak no more

Grieve you not
If I should die in your arms
Loving each as we do
Our life will be
An endless journey of joy

Pathway of Poems

LOVE ME OR NOT

Oh, no
How do I
I still am waiting
For one of only you
Love you solely
With all my being

Radiant in grace
That Nature envies
Keep on loving me
A kiss here
A kiss there
Shyly if you could
I settle for it
I know you more than
You ever know yourself

I adore thee
For how you are
Not for what you are
You swore to tell me
If you care for me
Oh, why me for you
Call it my fortune

Love me or not
I know thy heart
Love thee I must
Or I perish

Pathway of Poems

SHE IS it, NOT IT

She is in death dying
Goodbye yet unsaid
She was She
Now She is "it", not "IT"
She knew she became "it"
IT was hers to own
IT was her persona
IT was hers to command
She knew
IT and it will soon part
Not know how or when
Chose not to ask why
For She knew well
The fragrance of life
Lived yesterday

She is a non-person
It is voiceless
It lays motionless
Viewless of the world
Soulless if you will
It does not know her
Does not fit her
Not sing her songs
Nor air her persona

When she was She
She knew
Life will move on
To pass this way again

Pathway of Poems

ODE TO MY WIFE
(Jaya)

Thy name says it all
Glory and victory
Personable and gentle
Patient and caring
She comes into our life
A venerable woman
A devout mother driven to serve
In daily life, toil tirelessly
Not for wanted-ness
Just to be there for children
Has no time of own
All given to kids who forever are

A selfless soul with a restless mind
Filled with compassion, ponders over
What else to kids
It remains forever "the unfinished"

Nobody knows all she does
Busy as a bee
Breakfast in car ride
A norm for any day
Drop kids off at school
Copy homework when
School closing bell rings
Never miss to tuck each one to bed
Never miss to read stories or sing lullaby
Sweet as a flower does all with a smile

That is not the full story
Her husband of five decades
Is no less a kid to love and to be loved
A kid to care, keep him alive
His heart beating

Pathway of Poems

Need I say more?
A voice of reason, nothing goes undone
Cooking to coaxing to feed
Missing buttons to mending crotches
Sweaters for gifts, Afghan for college kids
All leisure consumed, she never knew it

A doctor at home with versatile talent
One of a kind none could excel
Medicine woman to friends and neighbors
Surgical suturing for son
Setting daughter's fractured toe
Doctor's scripts free to heal others

Sweet mellowed voice
One of classical music, another of robust
Love and compassion, values and virtues
Spring from her mold
Make a life, not a living, her motto

Humane and forgiving
Stricken by conviction
In the goodness of all
Never unfeeling or cease to agonize
Over ills of the world
Blessed, one like her crossed our path

Prayers never ceased
Tears of worship for dark hours or illness
Day never ends, body never rests
Now you know
What is so great about her

Selfless in grace and beauty
Dances the waltz of life

Pathway of Poems

BIRTHDAY GREETINGS

Greetings came in
For seven ten and five
My mind strolling
Why all the fuss in kind

A year is just over
Full of awe and glee
Glad, am I not?
Life seems
An incense in the air
Coasting to land

Withered many miles
Less a mile to go
It smiles on my lips
Dare I say I miss
Or dare I say I kiss
One more mirage-mile
How of it I see
More to dream on
To miles ahead
Than hold on to
Miles gone past
Just one mirage-mile
Is all if I could ask

Pathway of Poems

WHEN IT IS NOT, IT IS

When people say

It is not about money
It is

It is not what you think
It is

It is not how it looks
It is

It is not you
It is

It is not fair
It is

It is not fear of death
It is

It is not to punish
It is

It is not who you are
It is

It is not what I mean
It is

When people say "not"
Wonder if they mean "is"
Begging the question?

Pathway of Poems

PSYCHIC AUTOPSY

Pundits pulsate
Penetrate and plow
My body and verses
Not the Psyche or
The life that was
With me all my life
Dissect the man
Mine his mind
And life after
Breath is gone

Could you see
Grace and beauty
Apart the dancer
If in ecstasy I dance?

Psychic autopsy
When I am tranquil
In final departure
Of what worth is it
For you or me?

Pathway of Poems

I SPOKE TO GOD

With reverence
Hope and faith
Stood in prayer
To speak to God
He never appeared
Nor heard my voice
Wondered if He is
In truth illusory

As I lay laboring
Real over fear
I heard a whisper
Of soul beneath
My brawny body
Rid of jitters
Transcend reality

I never knew
Soul and God
As not two
One or not one
But remained stoic
All that I am, One
In heart and soul
While I spoke
To God within

Pathway of Poems

DOORBELL COULD SPEAK

The doorbell could speak
Be witness
To my hearts echo
Time could redeem
Be witness
To memory stream
I don't speak of
The perfume of flowers
We missed to smell
The bee on your bonnet
We failed to see

The day never ended
We strolled endless
The Longwood Gardens
Hand in hand
Tangled in each
Eyes locked, hearts open
A flock of blue birds
Flew out cooing merrily

Could they be yapping
Of our budding love
Could you believe
They blurt out
My feelings in hide
Call it what you will
If love, I love it
I live it; you in it

Pathway of Poems

SOUND OF SILENCE

Sound of silence
Is all have you
When I no longer am
In body flesh

Voice is gone
The sound of me
In words and songs
All too familiar
Simmer in memory
Shared life remains

My thoughts
You read clear
Do not appear
Like spring flowers
Body and flesh gone
There I am still
Heart fused in
Out with you

More performed
Than we dreamed
Sense or non-sense
Let us laugh and dance

Pathway of Poems

NEW YEAR JINGLES

A Year is down
More will descend
Upon you in time
One at a time
With fresh air of
Hopes and aspirations
Dreams and determinations
All rolled into one

Hold your dream alive
Through the year
Down to the last day
The best optimism for
A believer in dream
You love it, live it
And wake up in delight
Not in defeat
For a second chance
For a new taller dream
Yet for the year next

The past is fading
Would you like it frozen
Spring flowers have died
Not bloom again
Memory filled mind
Is yet scared of silence
Time walks with you through
A symphony of life
Some sweet, some not
At dawn of a New Year

Pathway of Poems

BEAUTY THAT I AM

The beauty that I am
Is not my fault
Why do you scare me
Is that what you really are

On a magic string
You hold me scary close
Lest you may lose me
Often I called it quits
I couldn't go through with it
My love got in the way

You have me all to yourself
Does fear get in your way?
Don't go down that road
That is not who you were
Move away from it
Call me if you have to
Fill me in, tell me all you hear
When you hold my hand
For love or fear
It swells up my tears

You think beauty and sex
Never fail to mix, are lethal
Not for me, with a man like you
Beauty never made me a smug
Let me just be me for you

The beauty of my beauty
Is but a pain, not a gain
When it comes to men
Other than you, my man
You think I am all looks
There is more to me than
Beauty that so happened

75

Pathway of Poems

INTERNET WEDDING

Oh, my dear
Chatted on the net
Dated on chat
Net over person
Hitch is certain
Because fakes are
Spread on the net

Time seemed ripe
For the union
Internet Invitation
Followed by E-Vite
For all too familiar
Rehearsal Dinner
Set at Country Club
With a dress code
Fine and cool I said
No need to show up

Ordered a gift
Listed on Registry
Signed the Guest Book
My photo scanned
Counted me present

Room to room service
Better than Hilton
No packing, no travel
No jacket or tie
No hand shakes
I did from my room
Bless their "I do" on time

Pathway of Poems

WHISPERING TREE

It is trees, trees all the way
None listen to what I say
I may be small
Unlike a birch or banyan
But large in life
Never failed to save lives

Dressed in green
Million in all
Orderly in rows
Branch after branch
In cute shape and size
Quivering and hugging
Murmur secretly to each
As the wind shakes softly

Once a little sapling
I did not choose
To break loose
Rain and snow
Did the makeover
Cool and gorgeous

I breathe and sleep
Jiggle and jitter
Weep like a willow
Wake up as dawn glows

Not free of aging or disease
I am a desolate withering tree
Stripped of the million free
Each dropped on ground
I stand nude in beauty
Whispering if my folks
Gone in peace abode
Beneath on the ground, yet Above.

Pathway of Poems

I PRONOUNCE YOU

"I pronounce you"
He said….
Excited as I was
Ready to kiss my bride
I thought I faintly heard
The word "dead"
Instead "wed"
Wondered if dead
Missed target said

It wasn't
What I hoped
Puzzled, embarrassed
Witnessing the crowd

I said "no"
Tears in my voice

Talked to myself
"I can beat it"
I would break open
The gates of hell
Or heaven if it be
Jump off the cliff
Down on earth
At break of dawn
To the sound of
My village temple bells
Ring in the newly wed
Man and wife

Pathway of Poems

TIME SHALL FEIGN

I ask thee, Time
Show up slowly
Rainbow-like
A little latent
With passing time
Make room for brain
That it is, as is
In sluggish mode

Time shall feign
And reign
My tired brain
Unseeing what is on
Until it is just gone
I as you
Never kissed
What was missed

Persistent pain drops
Trickle down
In time release capsule
Keep me smiling
Ahead of pain
In deathless pursuit
Of pristine truth
Beyond our eyes

Pathway of Poems

ZEN TO FUN

Three scores and ten
Life in Zen
Filled with fun
Wasn't yet done

Gracefully walk out
The morning gym
Holding hands
Like never before
Lay eyes on each
Gleefully smiling
She stared
He stared
Feelings bubbled
Words stumbled
Two so tangled
All else felled

He spoke endless
Whisper proof mode
She missed every bit
Didn't mean to omit
Made up a recount
Belied his account
Nonetheless
He couldn't know
Nor could she
He gladly saw
Some thing from nothing

Pathway of Poems

That wasn't the fun
This son of a gun
Seemed good to go
Some more miles
On a familiar road
With a new mode

Never you could know
Thrills and fights
Songs and Sights.
Mature age brings
New visions, fears
With some tears
Of people you knew
Smells and tastes
Of uncooked food
Silent sounds
Ever rebound

What a world
We live in, I am amazed
Kaleidoscopic
Illusorily real
One life to live
Live it well

Pathway of Poems

DOORBELL IN DEAD DARK HOURS

In dead dark hours
Long after the sun had gone
Before the moon had shone
I made many, many visits
To kindle our love
And bundle up in bed

It is now my burden
My burden
To prove I am the lover
Who stole your heart
Trusted your "love smart"
Words of wisdom

Witness to my love
Is your tireless door chimes
That drew me into your arms
Every time I visited
If the doorbell could speak
Would I ask for whom else
The milkman or gardener
Did the bell ring

Even my terrier
A friend of this friendship
Knew well the happenings
Of love and romance

Don't you know
How often we sneaked
Into the garden behind
Strolled to the end of night's end
Until tears of joy died

Pathway of Poems

UNTIL I MEET MYSELF

Years come one at a time
They are headed down or up
I am not in touch
With the departure time
Nor is time in touch with me
The only known was
Time seemed more in control
Got me through by far
Nearer the destination
A mirage-like target

Direction was deceptive
Not upwards or outward
But valley to mountain top
Still seeking a direction
To discern
Not where I was
Or where I would be
But to who I am
Keep spinning on my axel
The Self I am as known
Self I am not as unknown
Fusion of non-self with self
Until I meet Myself

LABYRINTH
OF
LYRICS

Labyrinth of Lyrics

DOORBELL COULD SPEAK

Out in Longwood Gardens
Perfume of flowers I missed
But I missed to see
Bee in her bonnet kissed

A flock of blue birds
Flew out cooing merrily
If you call it love
I love it, live it, with you in it

Chorus

The doorbell could speak
Witness to my hearts echo
Time would be redeemed
Witness to memory stream

I always loved you
I give you proof when you want
The day never should end
Until the violets turn red

Out in Longwood Gardens
Perfume of flowers I missed
But I missed to see
Bee in her bonnet kissed

(Music CD available)

Labyrinth of Lyrics

HAUNT LIKE A GHOST

Promise of tomorrow
Is to me a sorrow
I open my heart to you
To share your wild dreams
For all my trust in you
You seem to care little
Why not give a piece of your heart
As token of your love

Chorus

You don't seem to know
I loved you more than I should
Are you a man of your word
Do you mean to love or lie

Did I mean any thing to you
I was hoping to join you
But don't read too much into it
It will haunt you like a ghost

Verse

Did you say now or never
I am no desperate girl
Do I smell some thing
Don't tell me
It is not what I think
It is not how it looks
If you risk playing this game
It will sting like a bee
Haunt like a ghost

Labyrinth of Lyrics

YOU CROSSED A LIMIT

All night long I lay on a sofa bed
With my eyes locked on the door
I waited to kiss you good night
It was a night of a long wait

I had a drink, dozed off living dead
When I woke up from a dream
I saw you kiss my friend on lips
Leaving a lasting taste as your tips

Chorus

Of the many nights I stayed late
This night has sealed my fate
Love is love, betrayed or loyal
But this love is going no where

I have been true to you all my life
You would have made a wonderful wife
Have I been so wrong for you, babe
He couldn't be the gentleman I was
Honey, this time you crossed a limit

Verse

He was not your man to kiss
What about me you seem to miss
I am not a prisoner of love any more
No more I could love you, I swear

How could you betray a good man
I don't know if this was your plan
I want to leave you alone
And let you and the other man
Live happily ever after
If there is such a thing waiting for you

Labyrinth of Lyrics

MY DAYS AS A LOVER

I can't ask you
To wait any longer
My interests are taking roots
You could find it amusing

I can't give the life you deserve
My days as a play boy is over
I am on a long pursuit
I am not a tyrant or rouge

Chorus

I hate to run away
Chasing my dream afar
You have a life to live
Look at me, a gentle deserter

What good will I be
If I can't be by your side
What a lover will I be
Not to kiss and cuddle

Verse

You have dreams too
I don't deserve you
If I can't share your life
Walk beside holding hands

I can't give you the love
The way I very much like to
I believe you deserve
A special some one in your life

Labyrinth of Lyrics

TASTE OF HEAVEN

I am madly in love
But together with you
I had been all alone
It was like hell for me
Had you been there
Hell would have been heaven
It is not easy for you to know
My love never stops for you

Chorus

I was down for days
Life was in shambles
Just being with you, honey
I see a heaven on earth
I would gladly wait
For as long as it takes
If I could have for ever
Is this the way every lover feels

Verse

Do you see what I see?
You and I sit and sulk
Is this love of lovers?
Are you and I lovers in hate or by fate
Could you not love me back
I hold you in my heart
Give me a part of your heart
I want a new beginning

Labyrinth of Lyrics

ALL IN THE NAME OF LOVE

I won your heart
I had you all for myself
You and I were Venus envy
Why now this strange idea
How could you feel less loved
I love you like a million
I would give all of me
Leave nothing to chance

Chorus

You are a man of high repute
Why this silly dispute
I don't know the basis
You don't like crisis
It is not so big a hitch
A girl like me can not patch
I want you back, my man
All in the name of love

Verse

Life in the past
Had gone on pretty smooth
Even true love has its troubles
My life has had its share
I wept for a time
Let it go; then I let it spur
Love between you and I
And got you smile again
All the way into my life

Labyrinth of Lyrics

DIAL ME FOR LOVE

You flip out for no reason
I am just the same guy
When I start to speak
You role your eyes

Could you look back
And feel how good I was
I meant a great deal
When I was young

Chorus

When you curl your lips
Your smile slips
I was darn good to you
Only man you ever had

Be it for love, be it for strife
Can't you let me be me
Do you mean to hurt
Or get close to flirt
Dial me for love in any case

Verse

Choose what turns you on
But let me be the man for you
All my love rained on you
Must sure open your heart

You know how good I was
Long before I met you
I am always here for you
Right when you heed

Labyrinth of Lyrics

NEVER TOO LATE

It is never too late
To get back to me
Don't blame it on fate
You stood by me even in crisis

Don't wait for tomorrow
To calm my sorrow
There is some thing about you
I can't live without for a day

Chorus

I never loved a girl
The way I love you
When I was low
You never struck a blow

You blew me away with your wit
I fell in love, not for nothing
That is what love does
That is who you are

Verse

Every thing felt so good
When you were with me
You held me with a charm
Made me smile wiping tears

Don't walk out on me now
And make it the story of my life
Lend me your love for now
Let me be your man again

Labyrinth of Lyrics

WITHOUT YOU

Truly I care for you
I ask you to live it right
Give me a part to shape it.
She managed to catch you
At that art I am no match
You have no clue who you are
You have no clue who she is
In time you must, you will

Chorus

I care but may be I shouldn't
If you have a girl or not
If you love me I am here
I want to be the girl in your life
I will give you my soul
Just for the asking
Without me you go hapless
Without you I go loveless

Verse

Don't you know
Any girl would love to have you
I feel I am already yours
Are you not mine to kiss
I am not hot or crazy
My love is pure
Sure to reach your heart
Look at me for a moment
You would see who you are
Right in my heart

Labyrinth of Lyrics

LOVE IS SO BEAUTIFUL

A wonderful life knocks on you
Why can't you be happy
I don't see you cheerful
Do you miss some thing special

I gave all there was to give
I could even die for you
What good would it do
I want to live for you

Chorus

Won't it be amazing
If a woman like you
Wanted more of me
Won't I be a blessed man

My love is so noble
My course is formidable
I am here to stay
I'm not going anywhere
Love is so beautiful

Verse

You have been special to me
Living had a meaning
Should you want some thing
I am ready for you

I can never let you go willingly
If you have to I can't hold you
My love will follow you
Until you and I are one

Labyrinth of Lyrics

GOOD MAN GONE WRONG

You have been good to me
Yet you keep me at bay
I want you to love me
I can't wait another day

You want to stay close
But you keep far away
You couldn't win my heart
How do I let you part

Chorus

If I bid you goodbye
Would it be wrong
Am I not better off
When you are gone
It is a rough road ahead
So don't you tell me lies
I'm better off alone
Good man gone wrong

Verse

Love's in your dream
A bright star in the night
You don't have to miss me
If you play your cards right

Just try to be a man
That is what I ask of you
Dream what you want to dream
Go wherever you have to

(Music CD available)

FELL IN LOVE INSTANTLY

Her beauty is unmatched
I fell in love instantly
She stood aloof sipping wine
None would dare to mix
I couldn't pass up a chance
I wondered about the risk
To ask or not to ask for a date

Chorus

She is all alone
Would she care for me?
I don't know if she has a man
Shame, she is all alone
One chance I have
I must try my luck
She is an amazing beauty
I fell in love instantly

Verse

I could not get over her
Since the day I met
Does she know how I feel
May be not
I don't care, I shouldn't care
Won't she like to be in love
I love her unashamed
That should tell some thing
Daringly I asked her out
I got my first date

Labyrinth of Lyrics

MY HEART HAS SPOKEN

All I get is a promise
Promise of tomorrow

I spent many nights
Sleepless nights, hapless days
No dream to dream
You got to love me deep
Or I got to keep
The one friend I have

Chorus

My heart has spoken
I am waiting
For days without a word
Life is short not to be happy

Love me deep or I got to go
I won't weep, not so my style
Wake up your love or I have got to go
I won't weep, that is not my style

Verse

Don't you drag it out
In hope of pleasing both
She too is a girl like me
Just be honest
The kind of man I like

Is it too much to ask
Make your choice soon
Or you may have neither
End up a man loving you

Labyrinth of Lyrics

ONE SILLY MISTAKE I MADE

The girl on the second floor
Was woefully lonesome
It is not what you think
Don't rush to say I got you

That is not what happened
You make me a sinner
Don't toss me out for now
That is not a deal breaker

Chorus

It is not a big breach
Love can not reach
Haven't I been faithful
Don't judge me in haste

You beat many moons
Of doom and gloom
You and I share a room
I never shared her room
One silly mistake I made

Verse

You know so much that isn't true
Why would you want to split
What ever happened, honey
To your mellowed moods
And pillowed whispers
I am puzzled, this isn't a game
Don't brand me a sinner for nothing
If what matters is love as it did
Don't give up on me

Labyrinth of Lyrics

I'll BET YOU LOVE ME

I still wait for your call
Have put my worries on hold
Bought you a blue diamond ring
The kind you always wanted

When you knock on door
I would have no tears to pour
You bet my words would fail me
But I wouldn't miss to kiss you

Chorus

I am in no grief or rage
Because you were gone a while
I have none but me to blame
My destiny was lame

You have a voice
Let me be your choice
Say what you like baby
I can't get over you
I'll bet you love me

Verse

While I was in slumber
You didn't run out of love
Your love took a little hike
Watched your pain from aside

I couldn't let go love on exile
I let none to fill your place
I dream a life with you
Don't you wait for another day

(Music CD available)

Printed in the United States
92975LV00005B/101/A